T0145026

We Can Walk Around with Everything

CAROLYN SINCLAIR MCCALLA

Illustrated by Kamar Thomas

WestBow Press books may be ordered through booksellers or by contacting:

WestBow Press
A Division of Thomas Nelson & Zondervan
1663 Liberty Drive
Bloomington, IN 47403
www.westbowpress.com
844-714-3454

ISBN: 978-1-6642-9567-4 (sc)
ISBN: 978-1-6642-9568-1 (e)

Library of Congress Control Number: 2023905073

Print information available on the last page.

WestBow Press rev. date: 04/10/2023

Dedication

For the little hearts hungry for everything.

A gift to

_____

From

_____

On

_____

"The thief comes only to steal and kill and destroy; I have come that they may have life, and have it to the full."

-John 10:10 NIV

New International Version (NIV)

Acknowledgements

All glory to Jesus Christ,
who has gifted me Himself
so that I can walk around with everything.

Carolyn Sinclair McCalla

Introduction

Dear Loved Ones,

Perhaps the most widely known of all Scriptures is that recorded in John 3:16, NIV, "For God so loved the world that he gave his one and only Son, that whoever believes in him shall not perish but have eternal life." It is the Gospel of Jesus Christ—the Good News—in 26 words.

It was placed upon my heart to share this good news in the form of a children's book, written early on the morning of February 23, 2016, on the final pages of my prayer journal. This is the book you hold in your hands. It seeks to share the Gospel of Jesus Christ and His pursuit of us—even unto death on a cross—in child-friendly language and vivid images. It seeks to boldly proclaim, "Because He lives we can live knowing, without a doubt, that we were made by Love, in Love, and for Love. We can walk around with everything!" That "everything" is the very presence of Jesus Christ within us.

This book has a place at bedtime story times, family devotions, children-centered Bible studies, and book clubs. Included are several resources to support children in uncovering the wonderful work of Jesus Christ on the cross. Please refer to the Reader's Guide, containing questions and graphic organizers to support engagement before, during, and after reading the book. Guidance is provided to encourage your child in an early Bible reading practice, along with a list of the Scriptures referenced throughout the book. These Scriptures may serve as an appropriate focus for subsequent children-centered Bible studies.

Praying that you read this with all the children you love, with great expectancy,

Carolyn Sinclair McCalla
Your Sister in Christ

Nya and Melba sat together, in the warmth of sisterly love, reviewing the day from sunrise to sunset.

"Today, I…" she began. "Today, I learned about the water cycle."

"The water cycle?" Melba asked.

"Yes. I learned that all the water that comes from the sky once filled the oceans."

"Ahh…"

"I love school because we learn the story of how things were born-like the rain. Where did I come from, Melba? How was I born?"

"Why sugah, you came from your Mom and Dad."

"But, where did Mom and Dad come from?"

"They came from their moms and dads," and anticipating her next question Melba said, "And their moms and dads had moms and dads, too."

"Okay, but how did we come from them?"

Melba sighed with exhaustion, "Well when their moms and dads met, they fell in love and did a special dance. Because they danced they made your parents, and then your parents met and fell in love and danced a special dance and had you."

"So all the people in the world were born because people really liked to dance?"

Melba chuckled, "No, not quite."

"In the beginning God, who is love, created all things."

"ALL?"

[1]"Yes, ALL. The sky, the two great lights to govern the day and the night, the waters teeming with life, the plants, the beasts that walk the earth, every living thing above and below-you and me. He made us in love, by love, and for love."

LET THERE BE

---
[1] Hear God speak it Himself! Read Genesis 1, & 2.

[2] "So because He is love, God made us in Himself, by Himself, and for Himself?"

---

[2] Hear God speak it Himself! Read Colossians 1: 16, & John 1:3.

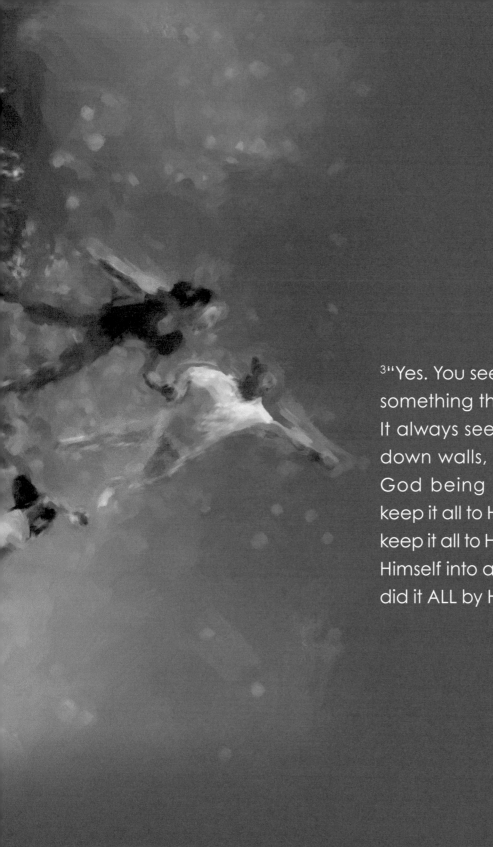

[3]"Yes. You see, love-real love-is not something that can keep to itself. It always seeks to share, to break down walls, to give of itself. And God being love itself, couldn't keep it all to Himself. Didn't want to keep it all to Himself, and so poured Himself into all of creation. And He did it ALL by Himself."

---

[3] Hear God speak it Himself! Read 1 Corinthians 13: 4 - 7.

"No help?"

"None. Love lacks nothing. And He didn't just make us and shelve us. You know, put us away or mount us like fancy toys. He made us so He could love us. He made us so He could relate to us."

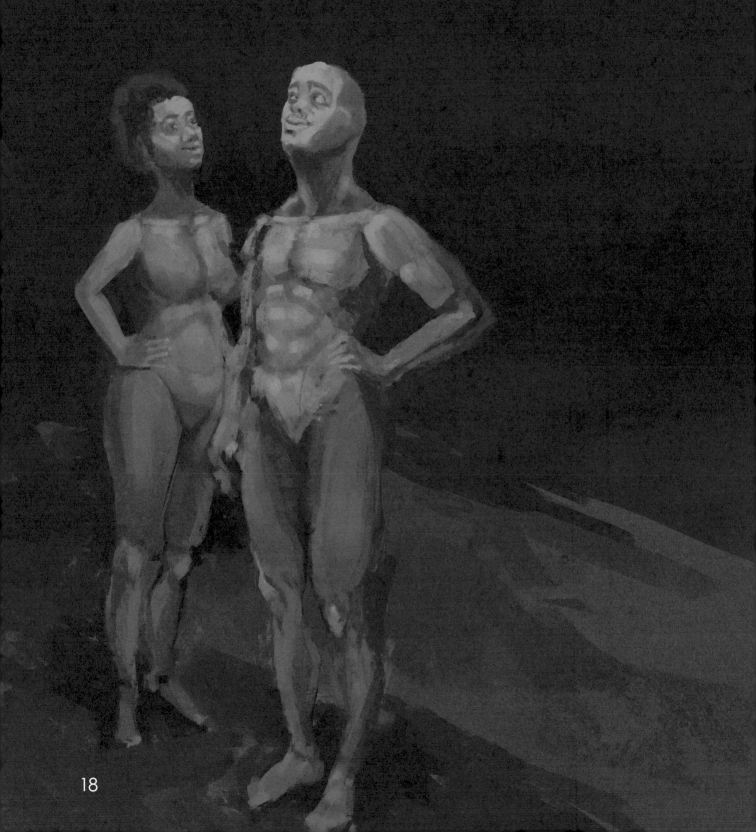

"Relate?"

"Yes, share with us. Like how we are sharing now, all nestled together by His love."

[4]"He made us just like Him: full because we had all of Him."

---

[4] Hear God speak it Himself! Read Genesis 1: 26 -28.

"Huh?"

"Remember, God is love and when you have love you lack nothing.
So, sweetpea, we had everything."

"But if we had everything, why do we walk
around now as if we have nothing?"

"Well, remember how I said Love breaks down walls?"

"Yes."

[5]"Well, sometimes Love puts up walls to protect, and God who is love put up a kind of wall: a rule to protect us. But we were curious and deceived by one who had no love. The one who had no love convinced us it would be okay to climb the wall Love built. We climbed and fell. Fell on the other side, far away from Love."

---

[5] Hear God speak it Himself! Read Genesis 3.

"Why didn't we just climb back over?"

[6]"Honey, because we broke into pieces when we fell. No strength. No nothing to build us up again. We were stuck on the other side with the one who had no love. Stuck for so long that we started walking around like we had nothing. Because without Love you are without everything."

---

[6] Hear God speak it Himself! Read Romans 1: 18 - 32.

"That must have broken God's heart?"

"It pained Him deeply. But, with love, there is always hope."

"What did He do?"

"He made a way for us to get over the wall, even though we were all broken up."

26

"How?"

"Well in order to get us back from the one who had no love, He had to pay a price. And the price was very high."

"Like a loving father who pays a ransom for the return of his child?"

"Yes."

"What was the price, Melba?"

"His Son's life."

[7]"God sent His Son to die for us?"

"Yes."

"Was it enough?"

[8]"Of course! Remember with love we lack nothing. We have everything. And Jesus Christ is just like His Father, who is love. The debt was paid! We **could** be free."

---

[7] Hear God speak it Himself! Read John 3:16, & 1 John 4:10 - 16.

[8] Hear God speak it Himself! Read John 10: 30 & 38, John 14: 6 - 11.

"Could?"

[9]"Yes. We **could** be free if we believed that God sent His Only Begotten Son, Jesus Christ, to die for us. If we believed that the payment was, is, and will always be enough. And that, though He died, He didn't stay dead, but is alive today!"

"Alive?"

[9] Hear God speak it Himself! Read 1 Corinthians 15: 3 - 8.

[10]"Yes, child. The one who had no love thought he had fooled God. But the one who had no love didn't understand the power of Love. Jesus Christ laid down His life for us and Love raised Him back up. And now He reigns forever! Because He lives we can live knowing without a doubt that we were made in Love, by Love, and for Love. We can walk around with everything!"

[10] Hear God speak it Himself! Read 1 Peter 3: 18 - 22.

31

"Melba, I want to be able to walk around with EVERYTHING."

"Pray with me child: Dear Heavenly Father, we thank you for your love for us. We thank you for sending your Only Begotten Son Jesus Christ to die for us. We thank you that we are now free because the payment was enough. We thank you that by your love, Jesus still lives today. Please come to live in our hearts today. In Jesus's name do we pray. Amen."

"Honey, now you've got everything."

Reader's Guide

Go on a picture walk of the book. What do you notice? What do you wonder? What predictions can you make about the book? You may use a table like the one below to record your thinking.

I Notice…	I Wonder…	I Predict…

During Reading

1. How does Nya conclude that "God made us in Himself, by Himself, and for Himself"? How does she figure it out?

2. How does Nya's sister describe Love?

3. Why does Nya's sister say God created us?

4. What do you think Nya's sister means when she says, "He made us just like Him: full because we had all of Him."?

5. Look carefully at the illustrations and use the clues to help you explain what Nya means when she says, "But if we had everything, why do we walk around now as if we have nothing?"

a.   What does she mean?

b.   How do you know?

c.   When does Love break down walls?

d.   When does Love put up walls?

e.   What makes the difference?

6.   Why did we decide to "Climb the wall Love built"?

7.   Why couldn't we just climb back over?

8.   How did God feel about our fall?

9.   What do you think God's response will be? What will He do?

10. How is God's response different or similar to what you imagined? Use a Venn Diagram like the one below to help sort the differences and similarities:

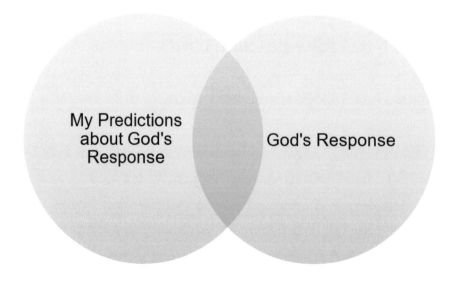

11. What does God's response tell you about Him?

12. Why does Nya's sister say, "We **<u>could</u>** be free" instead of, "We are free"?

13. How can we become free?

14. Do you want to be free?

After Reading

1. Based on what you have read, what have you learned about God? How would you describe Him? Use a table like the one below to help you!

God Did, Said, or Felt...	Therefore, I Think God is ...	I Still Wonder ...

2. Based on what you have read, what have you learned about how God feels or thinks about you? Use a table like the one below to help you!

God Did, Said, or Felt...	Therefore, I Think God Thinks I am...	I Still Wonder ...

Reader's Guide Continued

You have responsibilities when you have everything—Jesus. God, who is love, is always seeking to bring others into His perfect love. Now that you have God—your everything—you have to share Him! This is how we help the world become full again.

How will you share everything (Jesus)? With the support of your loved ones, look at the list of suggestions below, and commit to trying one, two, or all of them!

- **Gift this book** to a friend.

- **Gift this book** to a public library or church.

- **Host a book club** at your home with some of your friends. You could make yummy treats, read aloud the book with your friends, and then have your loved ones support you in going through the questions and related Scriptures in the Reader's Guide. You may have to meet more than once.

- **Create a piece of artwork** that invites others to walk around with everything (Jesus) and then share it! You could create a painting, poem, song, dance, etc.

- **Tell them about Jesus!** Walking around with everything (Jesus) is like walking around with a ball of sunshine in your heart. Everyone can see it. Every time someone asks you about your cheer or joy, be sure to tell them. He is the source of every good thing.

Reader's Guide Continued

This story is based on biblical truths that I encourage you to explore for yourself! Below is a list of key verses upon which this story was based. They are organized by topic.

These Bible verses are an excellent starting point for deepening your understanding of God's love for you and Jesus Christ's perfect work on the cross.

Before you get started, I suggest that you do the following:

- **Get your Word!** You will need a Bible. I suggest, "The Jesus Bible, NIV: Discover Jesus in Every Book of the Bible" by Zondervan because it includes helpful notes and devotionals to help you make the most of your Bible study by really putting the spotlight on Jesus! Your loved ones may purchase this Bible at any major book retailer. However, any Bible you have will do.

- **Get a journal.** The Word of God is unlike the stories you read for fun because it is living. Yes! You heard right. When you read the Word of God, it will talk right back to you. You may not hear an audible voice. However, it will speak to your spirit. Remember when Melba told Nya that God created us so we could relate to Him? Well, one of the most important ways God relates, or connects to His children, is through His Word. You will want to get everything He speaks to your spirit down. If He speaks it, you can be sure it is for your good. Note it!

- **Get a pen or pencil.** It would be pretty difficult to note all God says without a writing tool.

- **Get a quiet space.** God is very well-mannered. He really wants to speak to you, but He won't scream. Instead, He often chooses to whisper. Remember, you want to be able to hear what He is saying, so no distractions.

- **Get your heart right!** God is speaking all the time. However, we can't hear Him when our hearts are not right. Our hearts are not right when we are keeping our failures from Him. Hiding our shame, as Adam and Eve did in the Garden of Eden after eating the apple. Don't hide. Remember, God **really** wants to talk to you. Ask Him to search you and take away all the things that cause shame. Sin, which is disobedience to God, is always the source of shame. Pray this prayer of David recorded in Psalm 51:10, NIV, "Create in me a pure heart, O God, and renew a steadfast spirit within me."

- **Get into the Word!** You are all set to go.

- **Enjoy** the journey with the Father.

God is Love

- 1 John 4: 16
- 1 Corinthians 13: 4 - 7

God Creates & Purposes All Things

- Genesis 1 and 2
- Genesis 1: 26 – 28
- Colossians 1: 16
- John 1: 3

The Fall of Mankind

- Genesis 3
- Romans 1: 18 – 32

God the Father and the Son

- John 10: 30
- John 10:38
- John 14: 6 -11

Salvation: God Shows Forth His Love

- John 1:12
- John 3:16
- John 14:6
- Romans 5:8
- 1 John 4: 10
- Romans 6:23
- Romans 10:9
- 1 Corinthians 15: 3 -8
- Romans 5: 12 – 18

Printed in the United States
by Baker & Taylor Publisher Services